MW01139576

OUR FAVORITE BRANDS

TRANSFORMERS

By Emma Huddleston

Kaleidoscope
Minneapolis, MN

BIGFOOT BOOKS

The Quest for Discovery Never Ends

This edition is co-published by agreement between
Kaleidoscope and World Book, Inc.

Kaleidoscope Publishing, Inc.
6012 Blue Circle Drive
Minnetonka, MN 55343 U.S.A.

World Book, Inc.
180 North LaSalle St., Suite 900
Chicago IL 60601 U.S.A.

Kaleidoscope ISBNs
978-1-64519-022-6 (library bound)
978-1-64494-187-4 (paperback)
978-1-64519-122-3 (ebook)

World Book ISBN
978-0-7166-4322-7 (library bound)

Library of Congress Control Number
2019939235

Printed in the United States of America.

FIND ME IF YOU CAN!

Bigfoot lurks within
one of the images in
this book. It's up to
you to find him!

TABLE OF
CONTENTS

CHAPTER 1

Robots in Disguise

Ava and her dad went to see *Bumblebee.* It was the new Transformers movie. The main character was a girl named Charlie. Ava was excited that the star was a girl. Some people thought these movies were just for boys. They were about cars and fighting. Big metal robots clashed on screen. But Ava didn't care what people thought. She liked the robots and the stories.

People of all genders enjoy Transformers movies.

They bought popcorn and soda. Ava licked salt off her fingers. Her dad sipped soda loudly. The movie was a hit. It made more than $400 million. Ava's favorite part was when Charlie met Bumblebee. He was a cute yellow car. He turned into a robot in her garage.

Christina Hodson, who wrote *Bumblebee, was the first woman to write a Transformers movie.*

Ava's dad noticed something. The movie was more than big fight scenes. There were emotional moments. Transformers were for everyone. He finished his drink. The credits rolled. He saw that Christina Hodson wrote the movie. This was the first in the **series** written by a woman.

MOVIE AWARDS

Transformers movies have been nominated for many awards. They've won Teen Choice Awards and MTV Movie Awards. The movies have great special effects. *Age of Extinction* won a 2014 Hollywood Film Award for visual effects.

FUN FACT

In 2017, Transformers were nominated to be in the National Toy Hall of Fame.

Kids in the 1980s could watch Transformers cartoons and read Transformers comic books.

Ava's dad liked the movie. It reminded him of his childhood. He grew up in the 1980s. He watched Transformers cartoons. He read the comics. Bright colors covered each page. Some robots in *Bumblebee* looked familiar. He smiled. Maybe he would find his old comic books. He could show Ava.

FUN FACT

In the 1980s, there was almost a Transformers cereal, but it was canceled at the last minute.

CHAPTER 2

Transformers toys can be arranged as vehicles or as robots.

Transformers through Time

Takara was a toy company in Japan. It released a toy line in 1980. It was called Diaclone. The toys were **vehicles**. They could break apart. They snapped into different shapes. They turned into robots. Hasbro was an American toy company. It saw the Diaclone toys. It wanted to sell them in the United States. Hasbro worked with Takara. It renamed the toys Transformers.

Hasbro wanted the toys to have a story. It worked with Marvel Comics. Marvel writers created the robots' story. They gave each one a name and personality. Autobots were good guys. Decepticons were evil. The leaders were Optimus Prime and Megatron. The robots landed on Earth. They battled for many years.

The toys went on sale in 1984. So did the comic books. A Transformers TV series started that year, too. The brand was a hit. Kids loved playing with the toys. The robots became popular characters.

It was 1986. Pete went to see *The Transformers: The Movie*. It was based on the cartoon series. Pete watched the series every Saturday. He sat in his pajamas. He ate his cereal with milk. He had lots of action figures. Optimus Prime turned into a red-and-blue truck. Jazz became a race car.

Pete also loved the comic books. *Pow! Bam!* The robots fought on the page. Pete had every issue. He wished he lived in the United Kingdom. There was another Transformers comic book series there. That series was even more popular. For a while, more than 200,000 copies sold each week. Both series ended in the 1990s. Eighty issues were made in the United States. And 332 were made in the United Kingdom.

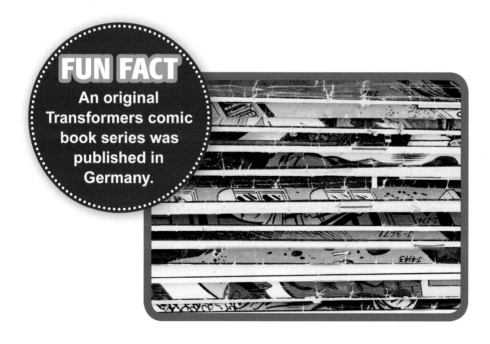

FUN FACT
An original Transformers comic book series was published in Germany.

TRANS FORMERS

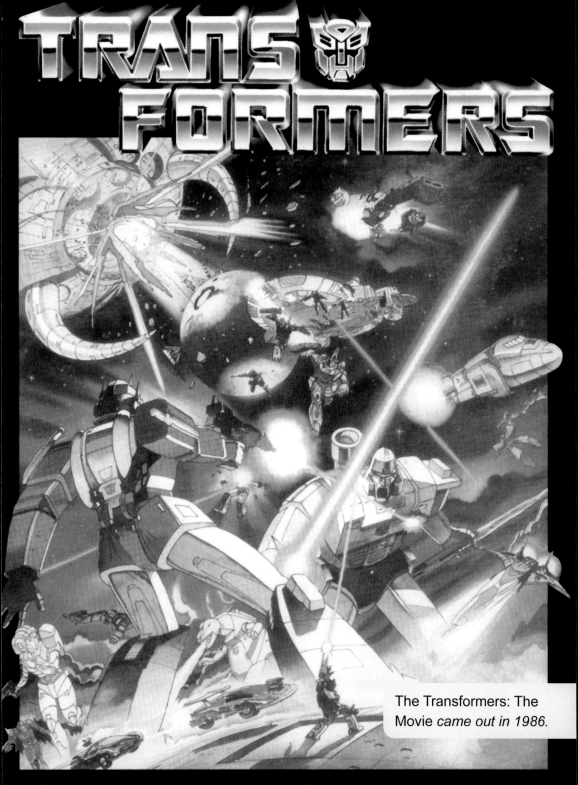

The Transformers: The Movie *came out in 1986.*

THE MOVIE

TRANSFORMERS
TIMELINE

1980
Takara releases
the Diaclone
toy line.

1986
*The Transformers:
The Movie*

| 1980 | 1983 | 1986 | 1989 | 1992 | 1995 | 1998 |

1985
The Transformers
video game is
released for
Commodore 64.

1984
The Transformers
toy line is
released.

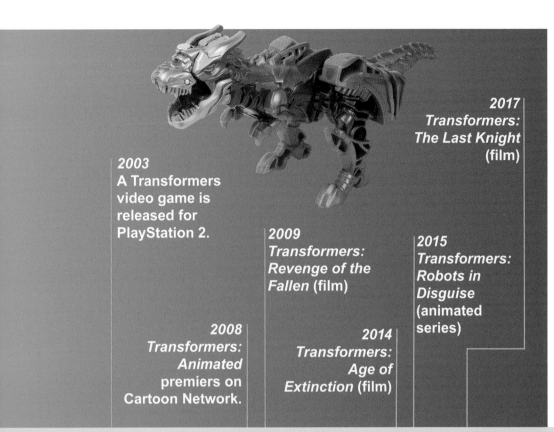

2003
A Transformers
video game is
released for
PlayStation 2.

2017
Transformers:
The Last Knight
(film)

2009
Transformers:
Revenge of the
Fallen (film)

2015
Transformers:
Robots in
Disguise
(animated
series)

2008
Transformers:
Animated
premiers on
Cartoon Network.

2014
Transformers:
Age of
Extinction (film)

2001   2004   2007   2010   2013   2016   2019

2007
Transformers (film),
Transformers:
The Game (video
game), and a new
Transformers toy line
are all released.

2011
Transformers:
Dark of the Moon
(film)

2016
Transformers:
Earth Wars
(video game)

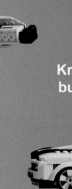

2011
Hasbro launches
Kre-O Transformers
building block sets.

2018
Bumblebee (film)

CHAPTER 3

In the Transformers movie series, Optimus Prime had a cool paint job when taking the form of a semitruck.

More than Meets the Eye

Matt went to the movies in 2007. He saw *Transformers*. He'd seen the cartoon. But this was different. This was the first Transformers movie with real actors. It brought the robots to life. The battle scenes were extra loud. Metal clashed. Robots fought with lasers and guns. Matt liked the movie. But he liked the video games more.

Many Transformers video games
have been released over the years.

In 2016, *Transformers: Earth Wars* came out. It was a mobile game. Matt downloaded it on his phone. He owned other Transformers games. He played them on his PlayStation. But this one was different. It had new robots. Two of them were twins. They turned into cannons. One was good. The other was evil. The game also had Combiners. Combiners were groups of Transformers. They joined to make bigger robots. Matt loved these new characters.

FUN FACT

Transformers: Earth Wars **was downloaded more than 10 million times in its first year.**

Liam wore a Bumblebee T-shirt. A Transformers notebook stuck out of his backpack. Action figures were scattered in his room. Liam got a Kre-O brick set for his birthday. He was building Bumblebee with yellow bricks. He could use those same pieces to make a car.

Hasbro released a line of Kre-O brick sets for building Transformers.

His sister Meg liked Transformers, too. She really liked when Transformers worked with other brands. In 2018, a comic book came out. It was *Star Trek vs. Transformers*. The series was inspired by the original comics. Meg loved the first issue. She couldn't wait to read the next ones.

TRANSFORMERS CROSSOVERS

Transformers have been in many crossovers. Hasbro released *Star Wars* Transformers toys in 2005. The mobile game *Angry Birds Transformers* came out in 2014. Transformers appear in comic books with characters from other franchises. There have been Marvel, *Star Trek*, and G.I. Joe crossovers. A Transformers-Ghostbusters comic book was announced in 2019.

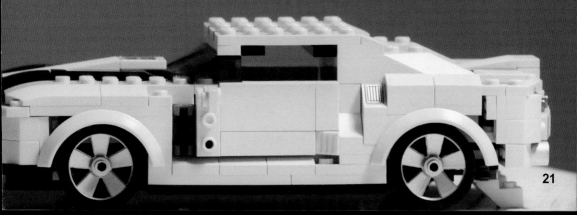

CHAPTER 4

Transformers around the World

It was 2014. Li Na and her brother got on the bus. They headed to the movie theater. They couldn't wait to see *Transformers: Age of Extinction.* Some scenes were set in China. Li knew the moviemakers had looked for Chinese actors. The search was aired on TV. They chose Li Bingbing and Han Geng. Hollywood star Mark Wahlberg would be in it too. He'd never appeared in the series before.

Li Na and her brother shared popcorn. The theater was crowded. The movie was a hit in China. It made more than $300 million there. It became the number-one film in Chinese history.

Transformers: Age of Extinction *did so well at the box office that it became the number-one film in Chinese history.*

Li Na and her brother went to the theater again three years later. They found seats. The theater was dark. They watched *Transformers: The Last Knight*. Optimus Prime had to save Earth. Earth began to combine with another planet. The movie ended on a **cliffhanger**! Li Na and her brother hoped the series would continue. They had to see what happened next.

Transformers: The Last Knight *came out in 2017.*

TRANSFORME
THE LAST KNIGH
FILMED WITH IMAX 3D CAMERAS
IN IMAX 3D, 3D & 2D THEATRES
COMING SOON

TRANSFORMERS MOVIES
AT THE BOX OFFICE

in the United States

The Transformers: The Movie $14.2 million

Bumblebee $127.1 million

Transformers: The Last Knight $131.1 million

Transformers: Age of Extinction $273.7 million

Transformers: Dark of the Moon $398.8 million

Transformers $418.1 million

Transformers: Revenge of the Fallen $485.7 million

Fin went to TFcon in Canada. It was the world's largest fan-run Transformers **convention**. Comic book writers spoke there. Fin watched the 1986 movie. Fin liked seeing the **collectibles**. Plastic-wrapped toys covered tables. He found an old Megatron toy. It was a fun weekend.

Daniel lives in Rhode Island. He plays basketball. His team has players with different abilities. They all work together to win. Daniel wants everyone to feel included. He won the Be Fearless, Be Kind award in 2018. It is an award from Hasbro and the Special Olympics. Hasbro is the company behind Transformers. It wants to encourage young people of all abilities in sports.

In the 1980s, Transformers made a splash. The robots were popular. They appeared on the screen and in stores. The brand has stayed popular over the years. It makes new movies, toys, comics, and more. This keeps the franchise fresh. Transformers have been around for more than thirty years. There really is more to these robots than meets the eye.

Transformers fans can find cool products and fellow fans at various conventions.

BEYOND

THE BOOK

After reading the book, it's time to think about what you learned.
Try the following exercises to jumpstart your ideas.

THINK

THAT'S NEWS TO ME. *Bumblebee* came out in 2018. It was different from other Transformers movies. Consider how news sources might be able to fill in more detail about the movie. What new information could be found in news articles? Where could you go to find those news sources?

CREATE

PRIMARY SOURCES. A primary source is an original document or object that was created at the time of an event or by someone close to the event. Primary sources include an interview with someone, videos or photographs, or writing from a diary. Create a list of the kinds of primary sources you might be able to find about Transformers.

SHARE

WHAT'S YOUR OPINION? The text states that Transformers movies are for everyone. Do you agree? Provide evidence from the text to support your opinion. Share your position and evidence with a friend. Does your friend find the argument convincing?

GROW

DRAWING CONNECTIONS. Create a diagram that shows and explains connections between Transformers and car parts. How does learning about cars help you to better understand Transformers?

RESEARCH NINJA

Visit *www.ninjaresearcher.com/0226* to learn how
to take your research skills and book report writing to the next level!

RESEARCH ···

DIGITAL LITERACY TOOLS

SEARCH LIKE A PRO
Learn about how to use search engines to find useful websites.

FACT OR FAKE?
Discover how you can tell a trusted website from an untrustworthy resource.

TEXT DETECTIVE
Explore how to zero in on the information you need most.

SHOW YOUR WORK
Research responsibly—learn how to cite sources.

WRITE ···

GET TO THE POINT
Learn how to express your main ideas.

PLAN OF ATTACK
Learn prewriting exercises and create an outline.

DOWNLOADABLE REPORT FORMS

Further Resources

BOOKS

Furman, Simon. *Transformers: The Ultimate Guide*. Revised ed., DK, 2007.

Scollon, Devra Newberger. *Transformers Planet Defenders Give Your Old Stuff the Reboot!* Curiosity Books, 2019.

Stewart, Melissa. *Robots*. National Geographic, 2014.

WEBSITES

FACTSURFER

Factsurfer.com gives you a safe, fun way to find more information.

1. Go to www.factsurfer.com.

2. Enter "Transformers" into the search box and click 🔍.

3. Select your book cover to see a list of related websites.

Glossary

cliffhanger: A cliffhanger is when a book, movie, or television show ends with problems left unsolved. *Transformers: The Dark Knight* ended in a cliffhanger and made fans want to see the next movie.

collectibles: Collectibles are items that people save for many years and that sometimes come in a series. Matt has many Transformers collectibles, such as action figures and old comic books.

convention: A convention is an event where a large group of fans come together to celebrate a brand or a group of related brands. The Transformers convention in Canada lets fans meet *Transformers* writers and actors, purchase products, and more.

franchises: Franchises are series of movies, TV shows, books, or other products about the same characters or universe. The Transformers franchise continues to grow with new movie, toy, and comic book releases.

nominated: Something that has been nominated for an award or honor was recommended to be on a list of potential winners of that award. Transformers toys were nominated for the National Toy Hall of Fame in 2017.

series: A series is a set of related books, shows, movies, or comics about the same story, characters, or universe. Many different Transformers series have been created since the toys were first released.

vehicles: Vehicles are modes of transportation such as cars, planes, and trains. Transformers change into vehicles.

Index

PHOTO CREDITS

The images in this book are reproduced through the courtesy of: Steve Heap/Shutterstock Images, front cover (Bumblebee); stefano carniccio/Shutterstock Images, front cover (background); Sittidej.K/Shutterstock Images, pp. 3, 14 (top); Image Source/iStockphoto, pp. 4–5; chingyunsong/Shutterstock Images, p. 5; Alex Millauer/Shutterstock Images, p. 6; Aisyaqilumaranas/Shutterstock Images, p. 7; DegasMM/iStockphoto, pp. 8–9; Sheila Fitzgerald/Shutterstock Images, p. 9; Geoff Caddick/PA Wire URN:7971271/AP Images, p. 10; BrendanHunter/iStockphoto, p. 11; Ryan DeBerardinis/Shutterstock Images, p. 12; Marvel Productions/Album/Newscom, p. 13; berni0004/Shutterstock Images, p. 14 (bottom); Red Line Editorial, p. 25 (chart); CTRPhotos/iStockphoto, p. 15 (top); Mark Lennihan/AP Images, pp. 15 (bottom), 20–21; Roman Korotkov/Shutterstock Images, pp. 16–17; Handout/KRT/Newscom, p. 18; Charles Sykes/Hasbro/AP Images, p. 19; SmileonBow/Shutterstock Images, p. 22; Rene Teichmann/Shutterstock Images, p. 23; Faiz Zaki/Shutterstock Images, p. 24; xactive/Shutterstock Images, p. 25 (popcorn); Stew Milne/AP Images, pp. 26–27; Marina Rich/Shutterstock Images, p. 30.

ABOUT THE AUTHOR

Emma Huddleston enjoys reading and swing dancing. She lives in the Twin Cities with her husband.